GW00706057

EUTHANASIA – NO!

A Joint Submission by the House of Bishops
of the Church of England and the Catholic Bishops'
Conference of England and Wales

CATHOLIC TRUTH SOCIETY
PUBLISHERS TO THE HOLY SEE
LONDON

First published 1993
The Incorporated Catholic Truth Society
38/40 Eccleston Square
London SW1V 1PD

ISBN 0 85183 892 8

Printed by The Ludo Press Ltd, London SW18 3DG

The Clerk to the Select Committee on Medical Ethics
Committee Office
House of Lords
LONDON SW1A 0PW   29 June 1993

Dear Mrs Ollard

The House of Bishops of the Church of England and the Catholic Bishops' Conference of England and Wales have agreed that they should make a joint submission to the House of Lords Select Committee on Medical Ethics. We have pleasure in enclosing the agreed text for consideration by the Select Committee.

There has been no opportunity for the joint submission to be considered by the Free Church Federal Council. However, a number of people from the Free Churches with expertise in this field have been consulted. It is clear that the joint submission would also receive the support of the Free Churches.

Yours sincerely,

Rt Revd Mgr Philip Carroll   Philip Mawer
General Secretary   Secretary General
Catholic Bishops' Conference   General Synod of the
  of England and Wales   Church of England
39 Eccleston Square   Church House
London SW1V 1PB   Great Smith Street
                                      London SW1P 3NZ

Revd David Staple
General Secretary
Free Church Federal Council
27 Tavistock Square
London WC1H 9HH

A JOINT SUBMISSION FROM THE CHURCH OF ENGLAND HOUSE OF BISHOPS AND THE ROMAN CATHOLIC BISHOPS' CONFERENCE OF ENGLAND AND WALES TO THE HOUSE OF LORDS SELECT COMMITTEE ON MEDICAL ETHICS

Foundations

1. The arguments presented in this submission grow out of our belief that God himself has given to humankind the gift of life. As such, it is to be revered and cherished.

2. Christian beliefs about the special nature and value of human life lie at the root of the Western Christian humanist tradition, which remains greatly influential in shaping the values held by many in our society. They are also shared in whole or in part by other faith communities.

3. All human beings are to be valued, irrespective of age, sex, race, religion, social status or their potential for achievement.

4. Those who become vulnerable through illness or disability deserve special care and protection. Adherence to this principle provides a fundamental test as to what constitutes a civilized society.

5. The whole of humankind is the recipient of God's gift of life. It is to be received with gratitude and used responsibly. Human beings each have their own distinct identities but these are formed by and take their place within complex networks of relationships. All decisions about individual lives bear upon others with whom we live in community.

6. For this reason, the law relating to euthanasia is not simply concerned either with private morality or with utilitarian approaches. On this issue there can be no moral or ethical pluralism. A positive choice has to be made by society in favour of protecting the interests of its vulnera-

5

ble members even if this means limiting the freedom of others to determine their end.

The sanctity of life and the right to personal autonomy

7. Attention is often drawn to the apparent conflict between the importance placed by Christians on the special character of human life as God-given and thus deserving of special protection, and the insistence by some on their right to determine when their lives should end.

8. This contrast can be falsely presented. Neither of our Churches insists that a dying or seriously ill person should be kept alive by all possible means for as long as possible. On the other hand we do not believe that the right to personal autonomy is absolute. It is valid only when it recognizes other moral values, especially the respect due to human life as such, whether someone else's or one's own.

9. We do not accept that the right to personal autonomy requires any change in the law in order to allow euthanasia.

10. The exercise of personal autonomy necessarily has to be limited in order that human beings may live together in reasonable harmony. Such limitation may have to be defined by law. While at present people may exercise their right to refuse treatment (although this may be overridden in special but strictly limited circumstances), the law forbids a right to die at a time of their own choosing. The consequences which could flow from a change in the law on voluntary euthanasia would outweigh the benefits to be gained from more rigid adherence to the notion of personal autonomy. But in any case we believe (para. 6) that respect for the life of a vulnerable person is the overriding principle.

11. The right of personal autonomy cannot demand action on the part of another. Patients cannot and should not be able to demand that doctors collaborate in bringing about their deaths, which is intrinsically illegal or wrong.

12. It would be difficult to be sure that requests for euthanasia were truly voluntary and settled, even if safeguards were built into the legislation, and not the result either of depression or of undue pressure from other people. Circumstances may be envisaged in which a doctor managing scarce resources might, perhaps unwittingly, bring undue pressure to bear on a patient to request voluntary euthanasia. Similarly families anxious to relinquish the burden of caring (or to achieve financial gain) might exert influence. Experience suggests that legislative change can lead to significant changes in social attitudes, and that such changes can quickly extend into supporting actions which were not envisaged by the legislature.

The distinction between killing and letting die

13. Because human life is a gift from God to be preserved and cherished, the deliberate taking of human life is prohibited except in self-defence or the legitimate defence of others. Therefore, both Churches are resolutely opposed to the legalization of euthanasia even though it may be put forward as a means of relieving suffering, shortening the anguish of families or friends, or saving scarce resources.

14. There is a distinction between deliberate killing and the shortening of life through the administration of painkilling drugs. There is a proper and fundamental ethical distinction which cannot be ignored between that which is intended and that which is foreseen but unintended. For example, the administration of morphine is intended to relieve pain. The consequent shortening of

life is foreseen but unintended. If safer drugs were available, they would be used: pain would be controlled and life would not be shortened.

15. Doctors do not have an overriding obligation to prolong life by all available means. The Declaration on Euthanasia in 1980 by the Sacred Congregation for the Doctrine of the Faith proposes the notion that treatment for a dying patient should be 'proportionate' to the therapeutic effect to be expected, and should not be disproportionately painful, intrusive, risky, or costly, in the circumstances. Treatment may therefore be withheld or withdrawn. This is an area requiring fine judgment. Such decisions should be made collaboratively and by more than one medically qualified person. They should be guided by the principle that a pattern of care should never be adopted with the intention, purpose or aim of terminating the life or bringing about the death of a patient. Death, if it ensues, will have resulted from the underlying condition which required medical intervention, not as a direct consequence of the decision to withhold or withdraw treatment. It is possible however to envisage cases where withholding or withdrawing treatment might be morally equivalent to murder.

16. The recent judgment in the House of Lords to permit the withdrawal of artificial nutrition and hydration from the PVS patient, Tony Bland, must not be used as an argument for the existing law to be changed. As with the general question of proportionate means, the complexity of the issue of artificial nutrition and hydration and the associated medical regimes means that there can be no blanket permission as regards PVS patients or those in a similar situation. At the very least, every person's needs and rights must be dealt with on a case to case basis.

The extent of the doctor's duty of care

17. The preceding paragraphs have touched on limits to treatment. The value attaching to human life implies that the primary duties of doctors are to ensure that patients are as free from pain as possible, that they are given such information as they and their carers request and require to make choices about their future lives, and that they are supported through the personal challenges which face them. We believe that to accede to requests for voluntary euthanasia would result in a breakdown of trust between doctors and their patients. Medical treatment might come to be regarded by the vulnerable person as potentially life-threatening rather than something which confers benefit.

The treatment of patients who cannot express their own wishes

18. Where formerly competent people have expressed their wishes about the way they would like to be treated, these should form an important consideration for doctors in determining how to proceed. Such wishes can only act as guidelines since medical conditions may exist for which they are inappropriate. If such wishes are unknown or inappropriate, or if a person has never been competent to express such wishes, then decisions about treatment should be worked out between doctors, families, carers and other health service personnel such as social workers or hospital chaplains.

Advance directives

19. Advance directives may be useful as a means of enabling discussion between doctors and patients about future treatment. Where they exist, they can only be advisory.

They should not contain requests for action which is outside the law, nor ask for the cessation of artificial nutrition and hydration. Care should be taken to establish that any advance directive was not made under duress. We would resist the legal enforcement of such directives since the medical conditions envisaged might be susceptible to new treatment, and medical judgments would have to be made about whether a person's condition was such as to require their advance directive to take effect.

Care of terminally ill people

20. The hospice movement developed from the concern of Christians that people should be helped to die with dignity. This work has enriched not only the lives of terminally ill people but also their carers, volunteers and health professionals, who have found that caring for those who are dying can be a great source of blessing.

21. We are concerned that the lessons learned in hospices about pain control, and emotional and spiritual support should be applied throughout the health service to all dying people. This requires that medical personnel remain aware of how advice on pain control may be obtained, and that adequate resources are made available for the care of sick and elderly people.

22. We believe that deliberately to kill a dying person would be to reject them. Our duty is to be with them, to offer appropriate physical, emotional and spiritual help in their anxiety and depression, and to communicate through our presence and care that they are supported by their fellow human beings and the divine presence.

Relevant Catholic Truth Society publications

Do 523   **Declaration on Euthanasia** *Sacred Congregation for the Doctrine of the Faith, Rome.* 5 May 1980

S 409   **Euthanasia** *Joseph Cardinal Bernardin, Archbishop of Chicago,* based on an address given to the Centre for Clinical Medical Ethics, University of Chicago Hospital, 26 May 1988

S 428   **Death – a friendly companion.** A pastoral approach to the dying and to those caring for them by Neil McNicholas. Includes a probably acceptable text of an 'Advance directive'.

Documents of the Catholic Church

The Catholic Truth Society, honoured by Pope Paul VI with the title 'Publishers to the Holy See', produces English versions of important Church documents as rapidly and as cheaply as possible. These include papal encyclicals and important statements issued by offices of the Roman Curia. The Society arranges to have these posted directly on publication to any address in the world.

The Pope Teaches

The Pope Teaches is a selection from the homilies and addresses of the Holy Father, in new English translations. Subscribers receive the text of speeches delivered to conclaves of cardinals and visiting pilgrims, to religious groups and secular organizations, to the Roman crowds and audiences abroad. *The Pope Teaches* is published monthly, and each issue is fully indexed so that the series builds up into a compendium of the spiritual wisdom, doctrinal teaching and social thought of Pope John Paul II.

Single issues £1.00

Annual subscription: UK £12
                       Eire £14
                       Rest of world £14

Irish subscribers wishing to pay in IR£ should allow for the exchange rate at the time and add the equivalent of an additional £1 sterling, which represents the bank's handling charge.

CATHOLIC TRUTH SOCIETY
38/40 Eccleston Square, London SW1V 1PD
Tel: 071-834 4392